**BOOK ANALYSIS**

By Steve MacGregor

# Little Women

BY LOUISA MAY ALCOTT

BrightSummaries.com

# LOUISA MAY ALCOTT

## AMERICAN WRITER AND POET

- **Born in Germantown, Pennsylvania in 1832.**
- **Died in Boston, Massachusetts in 1888.**
- **Notable works:**
  - *Hospital Sketches* (1863), collection of sketches based on letters written during the US Civil War
  - *An Old Fashioned Girl* (1870), novel
  - *Work: A Story of Experience* (1873), semi-autobiographical novel

Louisa May Alcott was an American novelist and poet, best known for her series of books based around the March family, the first of which was *Little Women,* published in 1868. She was raised by transcendentalist (a philosophical movement which started in the Eastern US in the 1820s) parents and educated by well-known intellectuals in her father's alternative educational school. Her family suffered financial hardship and she wrote and worked as a governess to support them. She remained single all her life and was a dedicated feminist and campaigner for the abolition of slavery.

# *LITTLE WOMEN*

## BE COMFORTED, DEAR SOUL

- **Genre:** coming-of-age fiction
- **Reference edition:** Alcott, L. M. (1868) *Little Women or, Meg, Jo, Beth and Amy.* Boston: Roberts Brothers.
- **1st edition:** December 1868
- **Themes:** women's roles, duty versus personal growth, the Protestant work ethic, the importance of family

This work was published at a time when the recent US Civil War had caused social and political upheaval and roles and expectations for women were beginning to change. Alcott herself had an alternative upbringing, but the traditional 19th-century Christian values of hard work, thrift and conformity are still present in her work.

*Little Women*, which takes place in contemporary America, tells the story of the genteel but impoverished March family: sisters Meg, Jo, Beth and Amy, their mother Marmee and their absent father. It tells the story of the sisters' growth into adulthood, as they face trials and challenges both personal and public and are visited by poverty, illness and death.

This book was extremely well received, becoming an instant classic, and it is still hugely popular amongst a mostly female readership today. This semi-autobiographical work was originally published as the first in a two-novel series, and Alcott wrote a sequel, *Good Wives,* which was published in 1869. In 1880, the text of *Little Women* and *Good Wives* was combined in a single volume which was also titled *Little Women*. In 1871, Alcott wrote *Little Men: Life at Plumfield with Jo's Boys.* This new book focussed on the character of Jo Bhaer (née March) and tells the story of the children at Plumfield Estate School. It includes several characters from *Little Women* and is regarded as the third (or second, if *Little Women* and *Good Wives* are considered a single volume) novel in the *Little Women* series. This was followed in 1886 by *Jo's Boys, and How They Turned Out: A Sequel to "Little Men"*, the final novel by Alcott to feature characters first introduced in *Little Women*.

This summary is based on the original 1868 version of *Little Women* and does not include *Good Wives*.

# SUMMARY

## THE FOUR PILGRIMS

The story opens on Christmas Eve with the four March sisters, Meg, Jo, Beth and Amy, complaining about their poverty. Their conversation reveals their characters. We learn that they are a respectable family who have fallen on hard times. They decide to buy presents for Marmee instead of themselves, and her return home with a letter from their pastor father who is absent while serving as a minister in the Civil War encourages them all to be positive. On Christmas morning, each girl wakes to find a copy of *A Pilgrim's Progress* under her pillow, and this book becomes a motif throughout the novel as they strive to bear their personal and external burdens as Christian does in the book. Later, they donate their breakfast to a poor family. Mr Laurence, their elderly neighbour, hears of this sacrifice and sends a huge meal over, and the day ends happily.

We are introduced to a close, warm and thoughtful family, guided by the calm centre of Marmee, who maintain their roles as impoverished gentlewomen with the Christian values of thrift, hard work and social duty central to their lives.

## THE LITTLE BROTHER

Later, Meg and Jo are invited to a party at a rich friend's house, where Meg revels in all the luxury and attention and Jo meets Laurie, the young and lonely grandson of Mr Laurence. They immediately become firm friends, a relationship that allows Jo to behave in a less ladylike manner than she is normally expected to do, and she later introduces him to the whole family, where he becomes an honorary son and brother.

Visiting Laurie whilst he is sick, Jo accidentally insults Mr Laurence, but he admires her spirit and later meets all the girls. He grows especially close to the shy and music-loving Beth, and sends her his dead granddaughter's piano as a gift.

## BUNDLES OF CONTRADICTIONS

We get to know the girls' evolving personalities through their various adventures. Meg and Jo must work to support the family because of their poverty, the former as a governess and the latter as a companion to the irascible Aunt March, whilst Amy and Beth aid Hannah, the help, to run the house. Romantic Meg dreams of a more comfortable life and Jo dreams of being a writer and having the freedom and independence to behave in a less ladylike way. Flighty and popular Amy, the artistic March, is caught trading limes at school, caned and withdrawn to learn at home. Jo and Amy fight because Jo will not take her along on a theatre trip with Laurie, and Amy retaliates by burning aspiring author Jo's precious writing. Jo has a temper that she finds hard to manage and she is so angry that she almost lets Amy drown when they are ice skating. Pretty Meg is taken on by a rich family and lets them dress her up in the latest fashion, but she soon feels uncomfortable and learns that appearances can influence the opinions of others. Gentle, domestic Beth, happy at home with her dolls and kittens, learns to fight her shyness at a picnic given by Laurie for some English friends where she chats to the crippled youngest son.

The family form the Pickwick Club and produce a family newspaper. Laurie is invited to become an honorary member, despite Meg hearing rumours that she wants to marry him for his money. Through these incidents, we learn of a family that works and plays together, that fights and makes up, whose moral compass revolves around the central tenets of family, respectability, hearth, and home whatever their differences, and whose lives are beginning to be affected by the outside world. At the centre of all of these happenings is Marmee, wise and loving with her advice and support as the girls struggle to shoulder their burdens, defeat their vices and come of age.

## THE LETTER

A letter arrives one day to say that Mr March is very ill in hospital. Marmee has to go and care for him and Jo cuts off her hair, her pride and joy, to help finance the trip. Accompanying her is Mr Brooke, the tutor of Laurie who has fallen in love with Meg. The sisters are left to cope alone but have many problems, with ruined meals and broken furniture. Little Beth falls seriously ill from scarlet fever, contracted from one of the destitute Hummels whom she visited when no one else would. Amy is sent to stay with Aunt March. Beth is ill for a long time and almost dies, so Marmee is finally sent for and she returns as the fever breaks, much to the joy of everyone. Beth recovers, though she never regains her full strength.

## ALL'S WELL THAT ENDS WELL

The book ends with Mr March returning home with his escort Mr Brooke, weak but content, and the family are able to celebrate together. Mr Brooke proposes to Meg with her parent's consent and she initially says no to him, but when the formidable Aunt March berates her about considering marrying a poor man, she changes her mind, and by the end of the book they are engaged.

Mr March gathers his family close in the parlour and he speaks of each daughter in turn, outlining the changes he sees in them, how he recognises how they have carried their bundles of burdens so bravely, how they have grown in to little women and fine ones of whom he is proud. The novel ends with another scene of warmth and togetherness, this time with a complete family around the fire, thus neatly bookending the story for the reader.

# CHARACTER STUDY

## MEG

Meg is the eldest and prettiest March sister. She is the archetypal genteel 19th-century girl with her love of fine dresses, nice food and frills and fripperies, and she is the only sister who can recall a family life when all of these things were readily available. She wants to be a wealthy woman and live in a beautiful house, and is a romantic girl, dreaming of dances and picnics. We are told that "She was 'fond of luxury' and her chief trouble was poverty" (Chapter 4, p. 58). This can make her greedy and sometimes jealous, and she spends a lot of time trying to become like her rich friend Sally Gardiner, allowing the Moffat family to dress her up like a doll in a manner unbecoming to her place as a respectable Protestant young woman. This opens her eyes to the fact that she does not feel comfortable like this. She is also a hard worker, serving as a governess to small children, and by the end of the book she is engaged to the poor but dependable tutor, Mr Brooke.

## JO

Jo is the character most similar to the writer herself: she is a tomboy, an aspiring author, clumsy, quick-tempered, adventurous and very unconventional. She wants to play with the boys and fight in the war with her father, and she generally subverts the contemporary notions of genteel womanhood.

At one point, she says "Mercy me! I don't know anything about love and such nonsense!" (Chapter 20, p. 294). Even her name, Jo, is the masculine form of her real name, Josephine. However, she also works hard, serving as a companion to the fearful Aunt March in order to help support her family. Jo eschews the idea of marriage and wants to do something great when she grows up, preferably with her 'scribbling'. Jo has to overcome her impulsivity and hot temper, and balance her ambitions with the expectations that come with her social role. She is a fascinating character and one that still resonates with readers today.

## BETH

Beth is almost unnaturally sweet, patient and angelic in a 'Tiny Tim' way, and we feel that she is not of this world, or at least not long for it (and these feelings prove to be correct in *Good Wives)*. She is too shy to go to school, so does a few lessons at home, but mostly fulfils the household chores and takes care of the little things that make life comfortable for her family. Content with her cats, her dolls and her music, she has no ambitions beyond the parlour. Her one luxury is the piano that Mr Laurence gives her, which once belonged to his dead granddaughter, a foreshadowing of what is to come. She becomes very sick as a direct consequence of doing good for others, and survives as an even more weak and ghostly presence. She is the classic "Angel in the House" figure epitomised in the eponymous poem by Coventry Patmore (English poet and critic, 1823-1896) – "She loves with love that cannot tire".

## AMY

Amy is the youngest of the four sisters. She is vain, affected, rather silly, pretty and popular at the start of the book, with ambitions to be a gentlewoman with all the trappings and the lifestyle that this entails. She hates the poverty in which the family is forced to live ("I don't think I *can* bear it, but I'll try", Chapter 17, p. 264), but she works hard on her appearance and manners, makes valuable social calls and is actually excellent at making social contacts. Amy is also artistic and has great natural taste. We see signs of a quick temper, such as when she burns Jo's story, and pique, as when she is punished at school and immediately persuades her mother to remove her forever. She is also a warm-hearted and honest girl, and this makes her popular in the social circles in which she moves. Her ambition to marry well is one which many young women in her situation would have understood and one of which her parents would have approved.

## MARMEE

Marmee is the perfect mother: she is hard-working, principled, socially active in helping others, a wonderful housewife and careful with the moral lessons she guides her daughters with. In fact, she is the idealised 19th-century Christian mother. She is strong under immense pressure and her religious faith guides and comforts her. She says: "I want my daughters to be beautiful, accomplished, and good; to be admired, loved, and respected [...] to be well and wisely married, and to lead useful, pleasant lives" (Chapter 9, p. 145). However, she has some unusual values in that she does not want her daughters to marry for money or status alone, and she gives them education and self-efficacy.

## MR MARCH

He is largely absent throughout the book and we only hear of him second-hand via anecdotes and letters. This allows the young women to take centre stage at a time when it was normal for the father to make all the decisions in the house. As a chaplain in the war, we learn that Mr March is kind, intelligent and courageous, and he sends advice and guidance to his daughters. Through his eyes, we see their progress and growth at the end of the book.

## THE LAURENCE CLAN

Mr Laurence is the Marches' wealthy elderly neighbour. Although he is supposedly difficult and intimidating, the girls soon melt his heart and he becomes a supportive and kind benefactor to them. His house has treasures that all the girls love: a piano, books, art and beautiful flowers. He keeps the story moving forward by giving the family money when they need it. Laurie, his grandson, is living with his grandfather as he is an orphan. He is rich, playful and the confidante of Jo, but a brother to all the March sisters. He can be moody and difficult, and has plans that do not match his grandfather's. He gives a masculine element to the book, being involved in many of the scenes and adding an extra narrative perspective. His tutor Mr John Brooke is a quiet, grave man, who is forced to work as he is also an orphan. He epitomises respectability in poverty, and even when he falls in love with Meg, he only approaches her after getting her parents' blessing.

# ANALYSIS

## THE TROUBLES AND TEMPTATIONS OF YOUR LIFE ARE BEGINNING

*Little Women* was written in the late 1860s as the first of a two-volume set commissioned at the behest of Alcott's publisher, and she needed to quickly draw readers into caring about all the March girls if the book were to be a success. Although it also contains aspects of romance and drama, this is fundamentally a coming-of-age novel. The characteristics of this genre include:

- a focus on the growth of the protagonists into adulthood;
- an emphasis on dialogue;
- internal monologues;
- the development of self-awareness through overcoming challenges and problems.

Alcott's writing has all of these elements. We follow the four March sisters as they move from childhood towards young womanhood, and the third person point of view enables the reader to follow each of the girls on their journey. The small town setting and limited action mean that Alcott has to use dialogue to illuminate the characters and their relationships. This also enables Marmee to give moral lessons and the girls to discuss their own progress and problems. Another characteristic of the coming-of-age genre present in the novel is the internal monologue, where the characters speak to themselves to describe their feelings and private dilemmas. For example, we learn of Jo's doubts about her writing ability and Beth's fear of people through their internal monologues. Finally, by the end of the book the four girls have shouldered their "burdens" (Chapter 1, p. 20) and come of age as wiser and more mature young women. Jo has learned to control her temper, Meg is less materialistic, Amy is less vain and Beth has accepted and worked on her shyness. Even Laurie has come to appreciate the love and values of his grandfather.

## WHO WILL YOU BE?

Contemporary gender expectations for women is a central theme in the novel, and the four

March sisters could be seen as representing four interpretations of 19th-century femininity. The dutiful Beth, the rebellious Jo, the creative Amy and the mother in waiting, Meg, are four women that modern readers instantly recognise. Whilst the societal constraints of the time limited what Alcott could represent women as embodying, there are also ideas here that would have pushed boundaries. For instance, Jo is a tomboy who wants to live an independent, unmarried life and Alcott specifically mentions creative, professional and unmarried women in positive ways, without denigrating the usual path for women of marrying for money or love. Closely related to this theme is the tension between duty and personal growth, and this is an idea that still resonates with modern women. The girls have duties which they must fulfil based on their religion, their gender and their societal status. They should care for others less fortunate than themselves, be seen to be genteel, perhaps marry well and for status, and do chores in the house, despite the fact that, as Amy and Jo epitomise, they would rather be creative, independent and explore other paths and talents.

## THE DEVIL WILL FIND WORK FOR IDLE HANDS TO DO

The girls try to find joy and fulfilment in their mundane everyday chores, and the importance of the Protestant work ethic is emphasised in the novel: "And prove that you understand the worth of time by employing it well." (Chapter 11, p. 173). Times when the girls do not work productively are shown to end up in chaos and personal disaster. For example, when Marmee lets them have as much free time as they want, the girls become bored and restless, and when Laurie comes upon them heading into the hills, he is only allowed to come if he promises to do something useful.

## WE ARE FAMILY

A further and central theme is the importance of family, again a reflection of the values of the time and of Alcott's personal experiences. The girls' character development takes place within their familial relationships, and it is through the eyes of each family member that we see the personal struggles and growth of the others. The main action and drama of the novel take place in a domestic setting, and we see the importance of a strong family, not just as an economically supportive structure but as an emotionally supportive one as well.

## THE VOICE

Alcott was a highly educated woman, and although the novel's setting may be cosy and domestic, she uses complex and challenging sentences and sophisticated vocabulary, whilst maintaining an easy-to-read style. She uses a lot of dialogue to break up the more difficult internal monologues, and each character has a clear narrative voice. Alcott displays a mastery of a range of literary techniques such as metaphor (for example, Jo's reference to "castles in the air", Chapter 13, p. 207 as a metaphor for the girl's hopes and dreams), allusion (for example, the girls call themselves "The Pickwick Club," (Chapter 10, p. 148), an allusion to *The Pickwick Papers* by Charles Dickens) and imagery (for example, fire is used as an image for several things including creativity and anger, as when Jo is described as "burning to execute immediate justice" (Chapter 21, p. 302)), which make the novel fresh and interesting. Although the language is very contemporary, with its use of embedded religious and moral lessons, it still resonates with readers today.

Much of the book is based on true events in Alcott's life. Her father was often absent and her mother was a central part of the lives of herself and her three sisters. Her father's transcendentalist beliefs offered an optimistic view of human nature, based on being true to oneself and not conforming. The family were genteel but poor, and she was educated at home, struggling to fulfil traditional female role expectations. Alcott became a staunch suffragist and believer in the abolition of slavery, and stayed single all her life. She herself served as a nurse in the Civil War, and was personally aware of the horrors and deprivations it caused. She was also aware of and active in the changing role of women, and her work reflected these concerns. Though traditional expectations of marriage, motherhood and domesticity still exerted a strong influence, moves towards emancipation were beginning, and she was very aware of the tensions for women that this involved. A woman could have domesticity or a profession, but to have both was difficult at that time. Finally, the Puritan and Protestant influences were strong in society as Alcott was writing. Each individual had duties and a work ethic and strived for respectability, and people lived by and were comforted by the moral precepts of the Bible.

# FURTHER REFLECTION

## SOME QUESTIONS TO THINK ABOUT...

- Many later editions of this work combined *Little Women* and *Good Wives* in a single volume. Do you think this approach works better than having this as a separate novel? Why/why not?
- How far are the archetypes represented by the girls in the novel still present in media representations of women today?
- In what ways does the novel support the idea of female conformity? Female change?
- Do you think the reader's gender would affect their appreciation of the novel? Why/why not?
- Why do you think that Alcott chose to make the father absent for most of the novel?
- "For conceit spoils the finest genius." (Chapter 7, p. 106). How far do you agree with this idea?
- Which character do you identify with most and why?

- Is modern family life in any way reflective of the life of the March family?
- Does the novel only resonate with white, Western readers? Explain your answer.
- How would the novel be different if it was narrated by one of the characters rather than by an omniscient third person narrator?

*We want to hear from you!*
*Leave a comment on your online library*
*and share your favourite books on social media!*

# FURTHER READING

## REFERENCE EDITION


- Alcott, L. M. (1868) *Little Women or, Meg, Jo, Beth and Amy*. Boston: Roberts Brothers.


## ADDITIONAL SOURCES


- Cheever, S. (2010) *Louisa May Alcott: A Personal Biography*. New York Simon & Schuster.
- Reisen, H. (2009) *Louisa May Alcott: The Woman Behind Little Women*. New York: Henry Holt and Co.


- This work is now in the public domain, and downloadable versions are available at Project Gutenberg at http://www.gutenberg.org/ebooks/514. This is the 1880 version which includes both *Little Women* (as Part 1) and *Good Wives* (as Part 2).
- The Internet Archive (https://archive.org) provides a scanned version of the original 1868 edition of *Little Women* at https://archive.org/details/littlewomenormeg00alcoiala.

# ADAPTATIONS

- There have been many film adaptations of this work. The first were two silent versions, both released during World War One. Subsequent English-language versions by major studios included releases in 1933, 1949, 1978 and 1994. In September 2018, a movie adaptation providing a modern re-telling of this story, *Little Women*, directed by Clare Niederpruem, was released to mark the 150th anniversary of the original publication of the work. In 2019, a new film version of *Little Women*, directed by Greta Gerwig, will be released.
- *Little Women* has also proved popular as a source for television adaptation. The first television version was an adaptation by NBC-TV in 1939. This was followed by other television adaptations in the US in 1946, 1949 and 1950. A musical adaptation created by the US broadcaster CBS was broadcast in 1958. *Little Women* has been adapted by the British Broadcasting Corporation (BBC) as a television series on four occasions, in 1950, 1958, 1970 and, in conjunction with the US Public Broadcasting Service (PBS), in 2018 to coincide with the 150th anniversary of the novel's original publication.
- *Little Women* has also been adapted as an anime series (twice), a musical, a ballet, an opera, several stage plays and an audio drama.

www.brightsummaries.com

Ebook EAN: 9782808015455

Paperback EAN: 9782808015462

Legal Deposit: D/2018/12603/531



Digital conception by Primento, the digital partner of publishers.

Printed in Great Britain
by Amazon

47150907R00030